KINDNESS

FR. FABER

SENSUS FIDELIUM PRESS

Gastonia, North Carolina

ISBN: 978-1-962639-92-7

For more information, please visit sensusfideliumpress.com

Nihil Obstat:

GULIELMUS CANONICUS GILDEA, S.T.D. *Censor Deputatus.*

Imprimatur:

HERBERTUS CARDINALIS VAUGHAN,
Archiepiscopus Westmonast.

CONTENTS

PREFATORY NOTE

Though it is not customary to prefix the memoir of an author to so small a portion of his works as the present, still the three decades of years that have elapsed since his death may have at least partially obliterated the memory of the great and gifted Father Faber. To prevent that memory fading from the minds of our young people this sketch is given. Those desirous of learning more of the illustrious Oratorian will find exhaustive details of his conversion to the Faith, etc., in his Life, written by the Rev. John Bowden, from which many of the facts of this memoir are borrowed.

MEMOIR OF
FATHER FABER

Frederick William Faber was the son of Mr. Thomas Henry Faber,
a Protestant gentleman of French descent. He was born at his
grandfather's residence, the Vicarage of Calverley, in Yorkshire, on
June 28, 1814. In the following year his father removed to Bishop
Auckland, where the family continued to reside till his father's death
in 1833.

Frederick, who was his mother's idol, was a singularly attractive
child, and gave early indications of the brilliant genius which
afterwards distinguished him. His parents, both of whom were people
of much intellectual culture, spared no pains to foster the nascent
talents of their boy, and were rewarded beyond their dreams by the
results.

After a brief sojourn at the Grammar School of Bishop Auckland,
Frederick was placed for a time under the tuition of the Rev. John
Gibson, at Kirkby Stephen. In 1825 he was removed to Shrewsbury
School. After a short stay there, he proceeded to Harrow, where he
remained till he entered the University of Oxford.

Whilst in Harrow, skepticism, then as now so rampant in England, had well-nigh dealt his spiritual being a deadly blow. God's merciful providence rescued him in the hour of danger.

He matriculated at Balliol College, Oxford, and came into residence there in 1833. One of his contemporaries writes: 'He resisted from first to last the temptations to which many succumb, and, by the grace of God, was able to preserve unstained the purity of his life.' He went to Oxford imbued with Calvinistic principles inherited from his parents, and treasured by him all the more in that he had so narrowly escaped the loss of faith in Harrow. After some months, however, Frederick's religious tendencies underwent a change. This change was brought about by the High Church movement, under the influence of which he had now to some extent fallen. For the leader of the movement, the illustrious John Henry Newman, afterwards Cardinal, Faber conceived an affectionate veneration which lasted through life. But whilst fully sympathizing with the spirit which animated this movement, he, nevertheless, shrank from the lengths to which some of its advocates were going.

That his earnest and deeply religious nature was even now striving after truth is evidenced in every page of the voluminous correspondence penned by him at this period. A few extracts from his letters may not be out of place here as showing the tone of his mind at this time. In a letter dated from the University in January 1835, he thanks God that the temporalities of the Church of England are no longer such as to induce men to enter the ministry from motives of mere worldly ambition.

To realize fully the disinterestedness of these views, we must bear in mind that from his earliest years his aspirations had all tended towards the clerical state. In a letter dated the same month and year as the above, he writes: 'I feel to an almost sinful degree that I never could be happy or content in any other profession. It has thrown a color over all my boyhood; it has been my life's one dream, so much so that I sometimes fancy I am called to it. So high, however, is the standard which I have set up in my own mind, and so much below that standard do I feel myself, that I do at times question my fitness for so awful a vocation.'

What wonder that the deep personal love of our Divine Lord, which even now is so apparent, should, increasing with his years, give him that wonderful success in dealing with souls which marked his missionary labors as a Catholic priest!

On May 26, 1839, he received ordination in Oxford, and soon after made a brief visit to the Continent, whence he returned very unfavorably impressed with what he had seen of Catholicism, a result, no doubt, of his prejudices against the faith. In 1840 he accepted the post of tutor to the eldest son of Mr. Harrison of Ambleside. The greater part of 1841 was spent on the Continent as travelling companion to Mr. Harrison.

Meanwhile prayer and spiritual reading had been doing their work in his soul, and it was from a different standpoint that he now studied the Church which he had recently regarded so unfavorably. Already the light of faith, under the touch of grace, was beginning to dawn upon his mind.

In 1842 Faber, after some hesitation, accepted the rectory of Elton, and on April 2, 1843, he introduced himself there. Next day, accompanied by his late pupil, he set out on his travels.

While in Rome, Dr. Grant took him to see St. Peter's. Writing of it, he says: 'The roof gives one the true notion of its enormous size; the cottages of the workmen, with the spacious offices, the fountains, and the whole appurtenances of a little village, seem only to occupy a moderate portion of the roof of a single church! The idea of people living, cooking, sleeping, etc., on the roof struck me beyond anything.'

On June 17, 1843, Faber had a private audience with the Pope, Gregory XVI. His Holiness, who was alone, said: 'You must not mislead yourself in wishing for unity, yet waiting for your Church to move.

Think of the salvation of your own soul.' After some further words of counsel, he laid his hands on Faber's shoulders, who immediately knelt down, upon which he laid them on his head, saying: 'May the grace of God correspond to your good wishes and deliver you from the nets of Anglicanism, and bring you to the true holy Church.' And for answer to the holy Pontiff's prayer, he had not long to wait. Gradually the veil was removed from his eyes, till at last he beheld in all her majesty and beauty the One, Holy, Catholic Church, the nursing Mother of the Saints, from whom all ecclesiastical authority emanates, whose Founder neither can deceive nor be deceived, Who will be with her all days, even to the consummation of the world.

While in Florence he began to wear the miraculous medal, and would have made a practice of invoking our Immaculate Mother were he not withheld from doing so by Newman, who disapproved of his taking so pronounced a step in favor of Rome whilst still fluctuating as to her claims on his allegiance.

It seems, indeed, certain that he would have entered the Church before returning to England had not Newman succeeded in dissuading him. He, who later on was to shed so bright a luster on the Church, was still undecided in his religious opinions, and resolved to make no move towards Catholicity till he had sounded to their depths the vitally important questions on which such momentous issues hung. He strongly advised his friend to do likewise, and the latter, in deference to the wishes of one whose counsels he had been accustomed to follow, consented to remain for the present in the Anglican communion.

On his return to England, Faber at once entered upon his duties at Elton. Notorious as they were for their callousness and indifference, his new flock afforded ample scope for the exercise of his zeal. Carefully avoiding controversy, he selected such subjects for his sermons as were calculated to instill a love and reverence for God and the moral life. Devotion to the Sacred Heart formed his favorite theme, as appealing to every denomination of Christians. Keeping his religious doubts in abeyance, the young pastor merged all his anxieties into zeal for the salvation of the souls confided to him. He visited the sick, consoled the sorrowing, taught the suffering to sanctify their pains by uniting them to those of our Divine Lord, and spared no effort to aid and encourage the faint-hearted in their striving after good. His utter unselfishness and entire devotion to their interests, combined with the unction of his preaching and his sanctity and austerity of life, soon obtained for him an absolute ascendancy over the minds of his people. The change wrought in them was marvelous. A number of his parishioners, especially the young men, began to come to confession to him weekly, and they frequently communicated.

In 1845 many of Faber's friends were received into the Church. Foremost amongst them was Newman. All his doubts dispelled, that great man, whose magnificent intellect, and spotless integrity of life were the admiration of Protestants and Catholics alike, brought with him to the Church a loyalty as unswerving as his gifts were great. Till now he had retarded Faber's conversion, but no sooner had he himself received the gift of faith than he hastened to communicate the joyful tidings to his erstwhile disciple, urging upon him the imperative necessity of at once making his submission to the Church of Christ.

Scarcely had the voice so long listened to as an oracle spoken in this sense than Faber's mind was made up, and he' resolved with as little delay as possible to enroll himself amongst the children of the Catholic Church.

On November 16, 1845, he officiated for the last time as Rector of Elton. At the evening service, after a few introductory words, he told his people that he could no longer remain in the Anglican Church, being convinced of its untenable position. Had a thunderbolt fallen amongst them, his audience could not have been more electrified. With saddened hearts, some bent their steps homewards, while others followed him to the Rectory, imploring him to reconsider his decision. On the following morning, November 17, he left Elton forever, accompanied by Mr. T. F. Knox, Scholar of Trinity College, his two servants, and seven of his parishioners, all of whom were to enter the Church with him. Loved and venerated as he had been by his flock, their grief at losing him was indescribable. Many, with streaming eyes and voices stifled by sobs, exclaimed: 'God bless you, Mr. Faber, wherever you go!' It was an hour of the most intense suffering for Faber; but the sacrifice was for God, and His servant counted not the cost. On that evening, he and his companions were received into the Church by Dr. Wareing, Bishop of Northampton. They made their First Communion and were confirmed on the next morning.

After a brief stay with his brother, Faber repaired to Birmingham on the invitation of the Rev. Father Moore and took up his residence at St. Chad's till he should come to some decision concerning the future. No sooner was he admitted into the Church than he began to devote himself exclusively to the furtherance of her interests. With the approbation of Dr., afterwards Cardinal, Wiseman, he took a small house in Caroline Street, Birmingham, and, with his eight Elton converts to form a community, of which he was Superior, took possession on December 19, 1845. From the moment of his conversion all Faber's aspirations tended towards the priesthood. October 12, 1846, December 19 of the same year, and March 20 following, were dates forever memorable to him. On these several days he received the Orders preparatory to priesthood, and on Holy Saturday, April 3, he saw the realization of his fondest hopes in the crowning grace of his priestly ordination.

He immediately received faculties to hear confessions and was entrusted with the sole charge of the Mission of Cotton. Overflowing with gratitude' to God, Who had dealt so tenderly with him,' all the energies of his being were devoted to the service of this good Master. He toiled incessantly to lead others to the truth.''' For this he preached, worked, and wrote. And when with fervid eloquence he cries out, 'Go and help Jesus: why should a single soul for which He died be lost?' he but gives utterance to the feeling that dominated his whole life, and which, united with a patience and kindliness that never failed, was the great secret of his success as a spiritual guide. We have already seen that he was a man of prayer, bringing everything, even his least important avocations, under its influence. Writing on the subject, he says: 'Intellectually speaking, it is very hard to believe in prayer; yet let us spend but one week in the real earnest service of God and the exercises of the spiritual life, and the fact, and far more than the fact, will lie before us, bright beyond the brilliance of human demonstration.' And again: 'All experience concurs with God's written word to tell us that the Immutable is changed by prayer.'

In 1847 Father Faber proposed that he and Father Anthony Hutchinson, who were the only priests in the community, should pronounce their vows as members of the Congregation of the Will of God, and he had written to Dr. Wiseman for the requisite permission. However, just at this time the news of Father Newman's projected return to England as Superior of the Oratorians reached him and suggested to him the idea of amalgamating the two communities. On February 14, 1848, they were 'admitted Oratorians.' Father Wilfrid, for such was his religious name, began his noviceship under the immediate supervision of Dr. Newman on February 21, 1848, and at the end of six months he was appointed Novice Master. The influx of novices was soon so great as to necessitate a removal to St. Wilfrid's, which was much more spacious than Maryvale. The number of subjects continuing to increase, Dr. Newman removed with part of the community to Birmingham, and opened a second house in London, of which he appointed Father Faber Rector; and when, in 1850, Newman erected it into a separate congregation, Father Wilfrid was elected Superior, a post which he held till his death. The present Oratory house at Brompton became the residence of the Fathers in 1855.

Father Faber's literary career, which began when he was scarcely twenty, was from the outset a most active one. But in 1853 he commenced a series of spiritual works, the first of which was 'All for Jesus.' This delightful book, so fascinating in style, so replete with instruction, was written in six weeks. It was followed in quick succession by Growth in Holiness,' 'The Blessed Sacrament,' 'The Creator and the Creature,' 'The Foot of the Cross,' 'The Spiritual Conferences,' 'The Precious Blood,' and 'Bethlehem.'

When we take into account Father Faber's duties as Superior, and the many calls upon his time from the thousands that sought his spiritual help, we are lost in wonder at the amount of work accomplished. But he was, in truth, an indefatigable worker.

Such constant application impaired a constitution never robust and engendered the germs of disease.

On November n he was summoned to Arundel Castle to attend the deathbed of Canon Tierney but had scarcely arrived when he was attacked with acute bronchitis. From this he recovered sufficiently to return to London for the celebration of the Feast of the Immaculate Conception. He wrote at this time: 'Pain does not altogether dispense either from penance or prayer... Ejaculations about the Passion and mental acts of conformity to God's will do me good.'

On April 23, 1863, there was a consultation of doctors as to his state, and their verdict caused grave uneasiness. On the 26th he said his last Mass, and on June 16 it was deemed necessary to administer to him the last Sacraments, as death seemed imminent; but he lingered till the end of September. For months his sufferings had been so intense that he had been unable to lie down. On September 25, his attendants, noticing a great change for the worse, placed him in bed. 'Here he lay supported by pillows, not speaking, but gazing steadily at a large white crucifix before him and moving his eyes sometimes from one of the Five Wounds to the other.... Just before seven o'clock a.m. a sudden change came over the Father; his head turned a little to the right, his breathing seemed to stop; a few spasmodic gasps followed, and his spirit passed away. In these last moments his eyes opened, clear, bright, intelligent as ever, in spite of the look of agony on his face, but opened to the sight of nothing earthly, with a touching expression, half of sweetness and half of surprise.' He was only in the forty-ninth year of his age.

The news of his death cast a gloom over the Metropolis, where he was mourned by thousands. Many lost in him a venerated father and trusted friend, whilst to countless souls his loss as a spiritual guide is not to be expressed.

Through life the kindness he has so eloquently advocated formed the keynote of his character. May the brightness of his example ever linger with us, that, won by its attractiveness and aided by its influence, we may strive to follow in his footsteps, however imperfectly.

Ursuline Convent, Thurles,
Feast of Our Lady Help of Christians, 1901.

ON KINDNESS IN GENERAL

The weakness of man, and the way in which he is at the mercy of external accidents in the world, has always been a favorite topic with the moralists. They have expatiated on it with so much amplitude of rhetorical exaggeration, that it has at last produced in our minds a sense of unreality, against which we rebel. Man is no doubt very weak. He can only be passive in a thunderstorm or run in an earthquake. The odds are against him when he is managing his ship in a hurricane, or when pestilence is raging in the house where he lives. Heat and cold, drought and rain, are his masters. He is weaker than an elephant, and subordinate to the east wind. This is all absolutely true. Nevertheless, man has considerable powers, considerable enough to leave him, as proprietor of this planet, in possession of at least as much comfortable jurisdiction as most landed proprietors have in a free country. He has one power in particular, which is not sufficiently dwelt on, and with which we will at present occupy ourselves. It is the power of making the world happy, or, at least, of so greatly diminishing the amount of unhappiness in it as to make it quite a different world from what it is at present. This power is called kindness. The worst kinds of unhappiness, as well as the greatest amount of it, come from our conduct to each other. If our conduct, therefore, were under the control of kindness, it would be nearly the opposite of what it is, and so the state of the world would be almost reversed. We are for the most part unhappy because the world is an unkind world; but the world is only unkind for the lack of kindness in us units who compose it. Now, if all this is but so much as half true, it is plainly worth our while to take some trouble to gain clear and definite notions of kindness. We practice more easily what we already know clearly.

We must first ask ourselves what kindness is. Words which we are using constantly soon cease to have much distinct meaning in our minds. They become symbols and figures rather than words, and we become content with the general impression they make upon us.

Now, let us be a little particular about kindness, and describe it as accurately as we can. Kindness is the overflowing of self upon others. We put others in the place of self. We treat them as we would wish to be treated ourselves. We change places with them. For the time self is another, and others are self. Our self-love takes the shape of complacence in unselfishness. We cannot speak of the virtues without thinking of God. What would the overflow of self upon others be in Him, the Ever blessed and Eternal? It was the act of creation. Creation was Divine kindness. From it, as from a fountain, flow the possibilities, the powers, the blessings, of all created kindness. This is an honorable genealogy for kindness. Then, again, kindness is the coming to the rescue of others when they need it, and it is in our power to supply what they need, and this is the work of the attributes of God towards His creatures. His omnipotence is forever making up our deficiency of power. His justice is continually correcting our erroneous judgments. His mercy is always consoling our fellow creatures under our hard-heartedness. His truth is perpetually hindering the consequences of our falsehood. His omniscience makes our ignorance succeed as if it were knowledge. His perfections are incessantly coming to the rescue of our imperfections. This is the definition of Providence, and kindness is our imitation of this Divine action.

Moreover, kindness is also like Divine grace, for it gives men something which neither self nor Nature can give them. What it gives them is something of which they are in want, or something which only another person can give, such as consolation; and besides this, the manner in which this is given is a true gift in itself, better far than the thing given. And what is all this but an allegory of grace? Kindness adds sweetness to everything. It is kindness which makes life's capabilities blossom, and paints them with their cheering hues, and endows them with their invigorating fragrance. Whether it waits on its superiors, or ministers to its inferiors, or disports itself with its equals, its work is marked by a prodigality which the strictest discretion cannot blame. It does unnecessary work, which when done looks the most necessary work that could be. If it goes to soothe a sorrow, it does more than soothe it. If it relieves a want, it cannot do so without doing more than relieve it. Its manner is something extra, and it is the choice thing in the bargain. Even when it is economical in what it gives, it is not economical of the gracefulness with which it gives it. But what is all this like, except the exuberance of the Divine government? See how, turn which way we will, kindness is entangled with the thought of God! Last of all, the secret impulse out of which kindness acts is an instinct which is the noblest part of ourselves, the most undoubted remnant of the image of God which was given us at the first. We must, therefore, never think of kindness as being a common growth of our nature, common in the sense of its being of little value. It is the nobility of man. In all its modifications it reflects a heavenly type. It runs up into eternal mysteries. It is a Divine thing rather than a human one, and it is human because it springs from the soul of man just at the point where the Divine image was graven deepest.

Such is kindness. Now let us consider its office in the world, in order that we may get a clearer view of itself. It makes life more endurable. The burden of life presses heavily upon multitudes of the children of men. It is a yoke, often of such a peculiar nature that familiarity, instead of practically lightening it, makes it harder to bear. Perseverance is the hand of time pressing the yoke down on our galled shoulders with all its might. There are many men to whom life is always approaching the unbearable. It stops only just short of it. We expect it to transgress every moment. But without having recourse to these extreme cases, sin alone is sufficient to make life intolerable to a virtuous man. Actual sin is not essential to this. The possibility of sinning, the danger of sinning, the facility of sinning, the temptation to sin, the example of so much sin around us, and, above all, the sinful unworthiness of men much better than ourselves — these are sufficient to make life drain us to the last dregs of our endurance. In all these cases it is the office of kindness to make life more bearable, and if its success in its office is often only partial, some amount of success is at least invariable.

It is true that we make ourselves more unhappy than other people make us. No slight portion of this unhappiness arises from our sense of justice being so continually wounded by the events of life, while the incessant friction of the world never allows the wound to heal. There are some men whose practical talents are completely swamped by the keenness of their sense of injustice. They go through life as failures because the pressure of injustice upon themselves, or the sight of its pressing upon others, has unmanned them. If they begin a line of action, they cannot go through with it. They are perpetually shying, like a mettlesome horse, at the objects by the roadside. They had much in them, but they have died without anything coming of them. Kindness steps forward to remedy this evil also. Each solitary kind action that is done the whole world over is working briskly in its own sphere to restore the balance between right and wrong. The more kindness there is on the earth at any given moment, the greater is the tendency of the balance between right and wrong to correct itself and remain in equilibrium. Nay, this is short of the truth. Kindness allies itself with right to invade the wrong and beat it off the earth. Justice is necessarily an aggressive virtue, and kindness is the amiability of justice.

Mindful of its Divine origin, and of its hereditary descent from the primal act of creation, this dear virtue is forever entering into God's original dispositions as Creator. He meant the world to be a happy world, and kindness means it also. He gave it the power to be happy, and kindness was a great part of that very power. By His benediction He commanded creation to be happy; kindness, with its usual genial spirit of accommodation, now tries to persuade a world which has dared to disobey a Divine command. God looks over the fallen world and repents that He made man. Kindness sees less clearly the ruin of God's original idea than it sees still that first beneficent idea, and it sets to work to cleanse what is defiled and to restore what is defaced. It sorrows over sin, but, like buoyant-hearted men, it finds in its sorrow the best impulse of its activity. It is laboring always in ten thousand places, and the work at which it labors is always the same—to make God's world more like His original conception of it.

But, while it thus ministers to Him as Creator, it is no less energetic and successful in preparing and enlarging His ways as Savior. It is constantly winning strayed souls back to Him, opening hearts that seemed obstinately closed, enlightening minds that had been willfully darkened, skillfully throwing the succors of hope into the strongholds that were on the point of capitulating to despair, lifting endeavor from low to high, from high to higher, from higher to highest. Everywhere kindness is the best pioneer of the Precious Blood. We often begin our own repentance by acts of kindness, or through them. The majority of repentances have begun in the reception of acts of kindness, which, if not unexpected, touched men by the sense of their being so undeserved. Doubtless the terrors of the Lord are often the beginning of that wisdom which we name conversion; but men must be frightened in a kind way, or the fright will only make them unbelievers. Kindness has converted more sinners than either zeal, eloquence, or learning; and these three lasts have never converted anyone unless they were kind also. In short, kindness makes us as Gods to each other. Yet while it lifts us so high, it sweetly keeps us low. For the continual sense which a kind heart has of its own need of kindness keeps it humble. There are no hearts to which kindness is so indispensable as those that are exuberantly kind themselves.

But let us look at the matter from another point. What does kindness do for those to whom we show it? We have looked at its office on a grand scale in the whole world; let us narrow our field of observation, and see what it does for those who are its immediate objects. What we note first as of great consequence, is the immense power of kindness in bringing out the good points of the characters of others. Almost all men have more goodness in them than the ordinary intercourse of the world enables us to discover. Indeed, most men, from the glimpses we now and then obtain, carry with them to the grave much undeveloped nobility. Life is seldom so varied or so adventurous as to enable a man to unfold all that is in him. A creature who has capabilities in him to live forever can hardly have room in threescore years to do more than give specimens of what he might be and will be. But, beside this, who has not seen how disagreeable and faulty characters will expand under kindness? Generosity springs up fresh and vigorous from under a superincumbent load of meanness. Modesty suddenly discloses itself from some safe cavern where it has survived years of sin. Virtues come to life, and in their infantine robustness strangle habits which a score of years has been spent in forming. It is wonderful what capabilities grace can find in the most unpromising character. It is a thing to be much pondered. Duly reflected on, it might alter our view of the world altogether. But kindness does not reveal these things to us external spectators only. It reveals a man to himself. It rouses the long - dormant self - respect with which grace will speedily ally itself and purify it by the alliance. Neither does it content itself with making a revelation. It develops as well as reveals; it gives these newly disclosed capabilities of virtue, vigor and animation. It presents them with occasions; it even trains and tutors them. It causes the first actions of the recovering soul to be actions on high principles, and from generous motives. It shields and defends moral convalescence from the dangers which beset it. A kind act has picked up many a fallen man who has afterwards slain his tens of thousands for his Lord and has entered the Heavenly City at last as a conqueror amidst the acclamations of the Saints, and with the welcome of its Sovereign.

It is probable that no man ever had a kind action done to him who did not in consequence commit a sin less than he otherwise would have done. I can look out over the earth at any hour, and I see in spirit innumerable Angels threading the crowds of men and hindering sin by all manner of artifices which shall not interfere with the freedom of man's will. I see also invisible grace, made visible for the moment, flowing straight from God in and upon and around the souls of men, and sin giving way and yielding a place to it. It is only in the deserts that I do not see it, and on the tracts of shipless seas, and the fields of polar ice. But together with grace and the Angels there is a third band of diminutive figures, with veils upon their heads which are flitting everywhere, making gloomy men cease to groan, lighting up hope in the eyes of the dying, sweetening the heart of the bitter, and adroitly turning men away from sin just when they are on the point of committing it. They seem to have a strange power. Men listen to them who have been deaf to the pleading of Angels. They gain admittance into hearts before the doors of which grace has lost its patience and gone away. No sooner are the doors open than these veiled messengers, these cunning ministers of God, have gone and returned with lightning-like speed and brought back grace with them. They are most versatile in their operations. One while they are the spies of grace, another while sappers and miners, another while its light cavalry, another while they bear the brunt of the battle, and for more than five thousand years they have hardly known the meaning of defeat. They are the acts of kindness which are daily enrolled in God's service from the rising to the setting of the sun; and this is the second work they do in souls to lessen the number of their sins. There are few gifts more precious to a soul than to make its sins fewer. It is in our power to do this daily, and sometimes often in a day.

Another work which our kindness does in the hearts of others is to encourage them in their efforts after good. Habits of sin, even when put to death as habits, leave many evil legacies behind them. One of the most disastrous parts of their inheritance is discouragement. There are few things which resist grace as it does. Obstinacy, even, is more hopeful. We may see floods of grace descend on the disheartened soul, and it shows no symptom of reviving. Grace runs off it as the rain runs from the roofs. Whichever of its three forms—peevishness, lethargy, or delusion—it may assume, God's mercy must lay regular siege to

it, or it will never be taken. But we all of us need encouragement
to do good. The path of virtue, even when it is not uphill, is rough
and stony, and each day's journey is a little longer than our strength
admits of, only there are no means of shortening it. The twenty-four
hours are the same to everyone, except the idle, and to the idle they
are thirty-six, for weariness and dullness. You may love God, and love
Him truly, as you do, and high motives may be continually before you.
Nevertheless, you must be quite conscious to yourself of being soon
fatigued—nay, perhaps of a normal lassitude growing with your years;
and you must remember how especially the absence of sympathy tried
you, and how all things began to look like delusion because no one
encouraged you in your work. Alas! how many noble hearts have sunk
under this not ignoble weariness! How many plans for God's glory
have fallen to the ground, which a bright look or a kind eye would
have propped up! But either because we were busy with our own work,
and never looked at that of others, or because we were jealous, and
looked coldly and spoke critically, we have not come with this facile
succor to the rescue, not so much of our brother, as of our dearest
Lord Himself! How -many institutions for the comfort of the poor or
saving of souls have languished more for want of approbation than of
money! and though sympathy is so cheap, the lone priest has struggled
on till his solitude, his weariness, and his lack of sympathy, have almost
given way beneath the burden, and the wolves have rushed in upon
that little nook of his Master's sheepfold which he had so lovingly
partitioned off as his own peculiar work! Oh, what a wretched thing
it is to be unkind! I think, with the thought of the Precious Blood,
I can better face my sins at the last judgment than my unkindness,
with all its miserable fertility of evil consequences. But if we have
no notion of the far-reaching mischief which unkindness does, so
neither can we rightly estimate the good which kindness may do.

Very often a heart is drooping. It is bending over itself lower and lower. The cloud of sadness thickens. Temptations lie all around and are multiplying in strength and number every moment. Everything forebodes approaching sin. Not so much as a kind action, not so much as a kind word, but the mere tone of voice, the mere fixing of the eye, has conveyed sympathy to the poor suffering heart, and all is right again in one instant. The downcast soul has revived under that mere peep of human sunshine, and is encouraged to do bravely the very thing which in despondency it had almost resolved to leave undone. That coming sin might have been the soul's first step to an irretrievable ruin. That encouragement may be the first link of a new chain, which, when its length is finished, shall be called final perseverance.

Few men can do without praise, and there are few circumstances under which a man can be praised without injuring him. Here is a difficulty. It is wise to take a kindly view of all human infirmities, but it is not wise to humor them in act. Some men can do without the praise of others because their own is so unfailing. Their vanity enables them to find self-praise sufficient. Vanity is the most comfortable of vices. The misfortune is, that nevertheless it is a vice. Some try to do without praise, and grow moody and critical, which shows their grace was not adequate for their attempt. Some do without praise because they are all for God, but, alas! it would not occupy us long to take the census of that portion of the world's population. Most men must have praise. Their fountains dry up without it. Everyone in authority knows this well enough.

He has to learn to praise without seeming to praise. Now, kindness has all the virtues of praise without its vices. It is equally medicinal without having poisonous qualities. When we are praised, we are praised at some expense, and at our own expense. Kindness puts us to no expense, while it enriches those who are kind to us. Praise always implies some degree of condescension, and condescension is a thing intrinsically ungraceful, whereas kindness is the most graceful attitude one man can assume towards another. So here is another work it does. It supplies the place of praise. It is, in fact, the only sort of praise which does not injure, the only sort, which is always and everywhere true, the only kind which those who are afraid of growing conceited may welcome safely.

Moreover, kindness is infectious. No kind action ever stopped with itself. Fecundity belongs to it in its own right. One kind action leads to another. By one we commit ourselves to more than one. Our example is followed. The single act of kindness throws out roots in all directions, and the roots spring up and make fresh trees, and the rapidity of the growth is equal to its extent. But this fertility is not confined to ourselves, or to others who may be kind to the same person to whom we have been kind. It is chiefly to be found in the person himself whom we have benefited. This is the greatest work which kindness does to others—that it makes them kind themselves. The kindest men are those who have received the greatest number of kindnesses. It does indeed sometimes happen, according to the law which in noble natures produces good out of evil, that men who have had to feel the want of kindness are themselves lavishly kind when they have the power. But, in general, the rule is that kindness makes men kind. As we become kinder ourselves by practicing kindness, so the objects of our kindness, if they were kind before, learn now to be kinder, and to be kind now if they were never so before. Thus, does kindness propagate itself on all sides. An act of kindness never dies, but extends the invisible undulations of its influence over the breadth of centuries.

Thus, for all these reasons there is no better thing which we can do for others than to be kind to them, and our kindness is the greatest gift they can receive, except the grace of God.

There is always a certain sort of selfishness in the spiritual life. The order of charity rules it so. Our first consideration is the glory of God in our own souls. We must take hold of this glory by the handle first of all. Everything will be presumption and delusion if it is taken in any other order. Hence, even while speaking of kindness, it is not out of place for us to consider the work which it does for ourselves. We have seen what it does for the world. We have seen what it does for our neighbors. Now let us see how it blesses ourselves. To be kind to ourselves is a very peculiar feature of the spiritual life, but does not come within our range at present. Foremost among the common ways in which kind actions benefit ourselves may be mentioned the help they give us in getting clear of selfishness. The tendency of nature to love itself has more the character of a habit than a law. Opposite conduct always tends to weaken it, which would hardly be the case if it were a law. Kindness, moreover, partly from the pleasure which accompanies it, partly from the blessing it draws down upon itself, and partly from its similitude to God, tends very rapidly to set into a well-formed habit. Selfishness is in no slight degree a point of view from which we regard things. Kindness alters our view by altering our point of view. Now, does anything tease us more than our selfishness? Does anything more effectually retard our spiritual growth? Selfishness, indeed, furnishes us with a grand opportunity of getting to hate ourselves, because of the odiousness of this self-worship. But how few of us have got either the depth or the bravery to profit by this magnificent occasion! On the whole, selfishness must be put down, or our progress will cease. A series of kind actions turned against it with playful courage, and selfishness is, I

will not say killed, but stunned, and that is a great convenience, though
it is not the whole work accomplished. Perhaps we may never come
to be quite unselfish. However, there is but one road towards that,
which is kindness, and every step taken on that road is a long stride
heavenwards.

Kindness seems to know of some secret fountain of joy deep
in the soul which it can touch without revealing its locality, and
cause it to send its waters upwards and overflow the heart. Inward
happiness almost always follows a kind action; and who has not long
since experienced in himself that inward happiness is the atmosphere
in which great things are done for God? Furthermore, kindness
is a constant godlike occupation and implies many supernatural
operations in those who practice kindness upon motives of faith.
Much grace goes along with kindness, collateral graces more than
sufficient in themselves to make a saint. Observation would lead us to
the conclusion that kindness is not a native of the land of youth. Men
grow kinder as they grow older. There are, of course, natures which
are kindly from the cradle. But not many men have seen a really kind
boy or girl. In like manner, as kindness in the natural world implies
age, in the spiritual world it implies grace. It does not belong to the
fervor of beginnings, but to the solidity of progress. Indeed, Christian
kindness implies so much grace that it almost assures the exercise of
humility. A proud man is seldom a kind man. Humility makes us kind,
and kindness makes us humble. It is one of the many instances in the
matter of the virtues of good qualities being at once not only causes
and effects together, but also their own causes and effects. It would be
foolish to say that humility is an easy virtue. The very lowest degree
of it is a difficult height to climb. But this much must be said for
kindness, that it is the easiest road to humility, and infallible as well
as easy; and is not humility just what we want, just what we are this

moment coveting, just what will break down barriers, and give us free course on our way to God?

Kindness does so much for us that it would be almost easier to enumerate what it does not do than to sum up what it does. It operates more energetically in some characters than in others; but it works wondrous changes in all. It is kindness which enables most men to put off the inseparable unpleasantness of youth. It watches the thoughts, controls the words, and helps us to unlearn early manhood's inveterate habit of criticism. It is astonishing how masterful it is in its influence over our dispositions, and yet how gentle, quiet, consistent, and successful. It makes us thoughtful and considerate. Detached acts of kindness may be the offspring of impulse. Yet he is mostly a good man whose impulses are good; But in the long-run habitual kindness is not a mere series of generous impulses, but the steadfast growth of generous deliberation. Much thought must go to consistent kindness, and much self-denying legislation. With most of us the very outward shape of our lives is, without fault of ours, out of harmony with persevering kindness. We have to humor circumstances. Our opportunities require management, and to be patient in waiting to do good to others is a fine work of grace. It is on account of all this that kindness makes us so attractive to others. It imparts a tinge of pathos to our characters, in which our asperities disappear, or at least only give a breadth of shadow to our hearts, which increases their beauty by making it more serious. We also become manly by being kind. Querulousness, which is the unattractive side of youthful piety, is no longer noticeable. It is alive, because an ailing or an isolated old age may bring it to the surface again. But kindness at any rate keeps it under water; for it is the high-tide of the soul's nobility, and hides many an unseemly shallow which exposed its uninteresting sand in early days, and will disclose itself once more by ripples and stained water when age comes upon us, unless we are of those fortunate few whose hearts get younger as their heads grow older.

A kind man is a man who is never self-occupied. He is genial, he is sympathetic, he is brave. How shall we express in one word these many things which kindness does for us who practice it? It prepares us with a special preparation for the paths of the disinterested love of God.

Now, surely, we cannot say that this subject of kindness is an unimportant one.

It is, as subsequent Conferences will show, a great part of the spiritual life. It is found in all regions, and in all of them with different functions, and in none of them playing an inferior part. It is also a peculiar participation of the spirit of Jesus which is itself the life of all holiness. It reconciles worldly men to religious people; and, really, however contemptible worldly men are in themselves, they have souls to save, and it were much to be wished that devout persons would make their devotion a little less angular and aggressive to worldly people, provided they can do so without lowering practice or conceding principle. Devout people are, as a class, the least kind of all classes. This is a scandalous thing to say; but the scandal of the fact is so much greater than the scandal of acknowledging it, that I will brave this last for the sake of a greater good. Religious people are an unkindly lot. Poor human nature cannot do everything; and kindness is too often left uncultivated because men do not sufficiently understand its value. Men may be charitable, yet not kind; merciful, yet not kind; self-denying, yet not kind. If they would add a little common kindness to their uncommon graces, they would convert ten where they now only abate the prejudices of one. There is a sort of spiritual selfishness in devotion which is rather to be regretted than condemned. I should not like to think it is unavoidable. Certainly, its interfering with kindness is not unavoidable. It is only a little difficult and calls for watchfulness. Kindness, as a grace, is certainly not sufficiently cultivated, while the self-gravitating, self-contemplating, self-inspecting parts of the spiritual life are cultivated too exclusively.

Rightly considered, kindness is the grand cause of God in the world. Where it is natural, it must forthwith be super naturalized. Where it is not natural, it must be supernaturally planted. What is our life? It is a mission to go into every corner it can reach, and reconquer for God's beatitude His unhappy world back to Him. It is a devotion of ourselves to the bliss of the Divine Life by the beautiful apostolate of kindness.

KIND THOUGHTS

Everywhere in creation there is a charm, the fountain of which is invisible. In the natural, the moral, and the spiritual world it is the same. We are constantly referring it to causes which are only effects. Faith alone reveals to us its true origin. God is behind everything. His sweetness transpires through the thick shades which hide Him. It comes to the surface, and with gentle mastery overwhelms the whole world. The sweetness of the hidden God is the delight of the life. It is the pleasantness of nature, and the consolation which is omnipresent is all-suffering. We touch Him, we lean on Him, we feel Him, we see Him, always and everywhere. Yet He makes Himself so natural to us that we almost overlook Him. Indeed, if it were not for faith, we should overlook Him altogether. His presence is like light when we do not see the face of the sun. It is like light on the stony folds of the mountain-top coming through rents in the waving clouds; or in the close forest, where the wind weaves and unweaves the canopy of foliage; or like the silver arrows of underwater light in the deep blue sea, with colored stones and bright weeds glancing there. Still, God does not shine equally through all things. Some things are more transparent, other things more opaque. Some have a greater capacity for disclosing God than others.

In the moral world, with which alone we are concerned at present, kind thoughts have a special power to let in upon us the light of the hidden God.

The thoughts of men are a world by themselves, vast and populous. Each man's thoughts are a world to himself. There is an astonishing breadth in the thoughts of even the most narrow-minded man. Thus, we all of us have an interior world to govern, and he is the only real king who governs it effectually. There is no doubt that we are very much influenced by external things, and that our natural dispositions are in no slight degree dependent upon education. Nevertheless, our character is formed within. It is manufactured in the world of our thoughts, and there we must go to influence it. He who is master there is master everywhere. He whose energy covers his thoughts, covers the whole extent of self. He has himself under his own control if he has learned to control his thoughts. The fountains of word and action have their untrodden springs in the caverns of the world of thought. He who can command the fountains is master of the city. The power of suffering is the grandest merchandise of life, and it also is manufactured in the world of thought. The union of grace and nature is the significance of our whole life. It is there, precisely in that union, that the secret of our vocation resides. The shape of our work and the character of our holiness are regulated from the point, different in different men, at which nature and grace are united. The knowledge of this point brings with it, not only the understanding of our past, but a sufficiently clear vision of our future, to say nothing of its being the broad sunshine of the present. But the union of nature and grace is effected in the world of thought.

But I will go even further than this and will venture to contradict a common opinion. It seems to me that our thoughts are a truer measure of ourselves than our actions are. They are not under the control of human respect. It is not easy for them to be ashamed of themselves. They have no witnesses but God. They are not bound to keep within certain limits or observe certain proprieties. Religious motives alone can claim jurisdiction over them. The struggle which so often ensues within us before we can bring ourselves to do our duty goes on entirely within our thoughts. It is our own secret, and men cannot put us to the blush because of it. The contradiction which too often exists between our outward actions, and our inward intentions is only to be detected in the realm of our thoughts, whither none but God can penetrate, except by guesses, which are not the less offences against charity because they happen to be correct. In like manner, as an impulse will sometimes show more of our real character than what we do after deliberation, our first thoughts will often reveal to us faults of disposition which outward restraints will hinder from issuing in action. Actions have their external hindrances, while our thoughts better disclose to us our possibilities of good and evil. Of course, there is a most true sense in which the conscientious effort to cure a fault is a better indication of our character than the fault we have not yet succeeded in curing. Nevertheless, we may die at any moment, and when we die, we die as we are. Thus, our thoughts tell us better than our actions can do what we shall be like the moment after death. Lastly, it is in the world of thought that we most often meet with God, walking as in the shades of ancient Eden. It is there we hear His whispers. It is there we perceive the fragrance of His recent presence. It is thence that the first vibrations of grace proceed.

Now, if our thoughts be of this importance, and also if kindness be of the importance which was assigned to it in the last. Conference, it follows that kind thoughts must be of immense consequence. If a man habitually has kind thoughts of others, and that on supernatural motives, he is not far from being a saint. Such a man's thoughts are not kind intermittingly, or on impulse, or at haphazard. His first thoughts are kind, and he does not repent of them, although they often bring suffering and disgust in their train. All his thoughts are kind, and he does not chequer them with unkindly ones. Even when sudden passions or vehement excitements have thrown them into commotion, they settle down into a kindly humor and cannot settle otherwise. These men are rare. Kind thoughts are rarer than either kind words or kind deeds. They imply a great deal of thinking about others. This is rare. But they imply also a great deal of thinking about others without the thoughts being criticisms. This is rarer still. Active-minded men are naturally the most given to criticize, and they are also the men whose thoughts are generally the most exuberant. Such men, therefore, must make kind thoughts a defense against self. By sweetening the fountain of their thoughts, they will destroy the bitterness of their judgments.

But kind thoughts also imply a contact with God, and a Divine ideal in our minds. Their origin cannot be anything short of Divine. Like the love of beauty, they can spring from no baser source. They are not dictated by self-interest nor stimulated by passion. They have nothing in them which is insidious, and they are almost always the preludes to some sacrifice of self. It must be from God's touch that such waters spring. They only live in the clammy mists of earth because they breathe the fresh air of heaven. They are the scent with which the creature is penetrated through the indwelling of the Creator. They also imply the reverse of a superficial view of things. Nothing deepens the mind so much as a habit of charity. A man's surfaces are always worse than his real depths. There may be exceptions to this rule, but I believe them to be exceedingly rare. Self is the only person who does not improve on acquaintance. Our deepest views of life are doubtless very shallow ones, for how little do we know of what God intends to do with His own world! We know something about His glory and our own salvation, but how the last becomes the first in the face of so much evil neither theologian nor philosopher has ever been able adequately to explain. But so much we are warranted in saying, that charity is the deepest view of life, and nearest to God's view, and therefore also not merely the truest view, but the only view that is true at all. Kind thoughts, then, are in the creature what His science is to the Creator. They embody the deepest, purest, grandest truth to which we untruthful creatures can attain about others or ourselves.

Why are some men so forward to praise others? Is it not that it is their fashion of investing themselves with importance? But why are most men so reluctant to praise others? It is because they have such an inordinate opinion of themselves. Now, kind thoughts imply a low opinion of self. They are an inward praise of others, and because inward therefore genuine. No one who has a high opinion of himself finds his merits acknowledged according to his own estimate of them. His reputation therefore cannot take care of itself. He must push it; and a man who is pushing anything in the world is always unamiable, because he is obliged to stand so much on the defensive. A pugnacious man is far less disagreeable than a defensive man. Every man who is habitually holding out for his rights makes himself the equal of his inferiors, even if he be a king, and he must take the consequences, which are far from pleasant. But the kind-thoughted man has no rights to defend, no self-importance to push. He thinks meanly of himself, and with so much honesty that he thinks thus of himself with tranquility. He finds others pleasanter to deal with than self; and others find him so pleasant to deal with that love follows him wherever he goes—a love which is the more faithful to him because he makes so few pretenses to be loved. Last of all, kind thoughts imply also supernatural principles, for inward kindness can be consistent on no others. Kindness is the occupation of our whole nature by the atmosphere and spirit of heaven. This is no inconsiderable affair. Nature cannot do the work itself, nor can it do it with ordinary succors. Were there ever any consistently kind heathens? If so, they are in heaven now, for they must have been under the dominion of grace on earth. We must not confound kindness and mere good-humor. Good-humor is — no! on such an unkindly earth as this, it will be better not to say a disparaging word even of mere good-humor. Would that there were more even of that in the world! I suspect angels cluster round a good-humored man, as the gnats cluster round the trees they like.

But there is one class of kind thoughts which must be dwelt upon apart. I allude to kind interpretations. The habit of not judging others is one which it is very difficult to acquire, and which is generally not acquired till late on in the spiritual life. If men have ever indulged in judging others, the mere sight of an action almost involuntarily suggests an internal commentary upon it. It has become so natural to judge, however little their own duties or responsibilities are connected with what they are judging, that the actions of others present themselves to the mind as in the attitude of asking a verdict from it. All our fellow-men who come within the reach of our knowledge—and for the most retired of us the circle is a wide one—are prisoners at the bar; and if we are unjust, ignorant, capricious judges, it must be granted to us that we are indefatigable ones. Now, all this is simple ruin to our souls. At any risk, at the cost of life, there must be an end of this, or it will end in everlasting banishment from God. The standard of the last judgment is absolute. It is this—the measure which we have meted to others. Our present humor in judging others reveals to us what our sentence would be if we died now. Are we content to abide that issue? But, as it is impossible all at once to stop judging, and as it is also impossible to go on judging uncharitably, we must pass through the intermediate stage of kind interpretations. Few men have passed beyond this to a habit of perfect charity, which has blessedly stripped them of their judicial ermine and their deeply - rooted judicial habits of mind. We ought, therefore, to cultivate most sedulously the habit of kind interpretations.

Men's actions are very difficult to judge. Their real character depends in a great measure on the motives which prompt them, and those motives are invisible to us. Appearances are often against what we afterwards discover to have been deeds of virtue. Moreover, a line of conduct is, in its look at least, very little like a logical process. It is complicated with all manner of inconsistencies, and often deformed by what is in reality a hidden consistency. Nobody can judge men but God, and we can hardly obtain a higher or more reverent view of God than that which represents Him to us as judging men with perfect knowledge, unperplexed certainty, and undisturbed compassion. Now, kind interpretations are imitations of the merciful ingenuity of the Creator finding excuses for His creatures. It is almost a day of revelation to us when theology enables us to perceive that God is so merciful precisely because He is so wise; and from this truth it is an easy inference that kindness is our best wisdom, because it is an image of the wisdom of God. This is the idea of kind interpretations, and this is the use which we must make of them. The habit of judging is so nearly incurable, and its cure is such an almost interminable process, that we must concentrate ourselves for a long while on keeping it in check, and this check is to be found in kind interpretations. We must come to esteem very lightly our sharp eye for evil, on which, perhaps, we once prided ourselves as cleverness. It has been to us a fountain of sarcasm; and how seldom since Adam was created has sarcasm fallen short of being a sin! We must look at our talent for analysis of character as a dreadful possibility of huge uncharitableness. We should have been much better without it from the first. It is the hardest talent of all to manage because it is so difficult to make any glory for God out of it. We are sure to continue to say clever things so long as we continue to indulge in this analysis; and clever things are equally sure to be sharp and acid. Sight is a great blessing, but there are times and places where it is far more blessed not to see. It would be comparatively easy for us to be holy if only we could always see the character of our neighbors either in soft shade or with the kindly deceits of moonlight upon them. Of course, we are not to grow blind to evil, for thus we should speedily become unreal; but we must grow to something higher, and something truer, than a quickness in detecting evil.

We must rise to something truer. Yes! Have we not always found in our past experience that on the whole our kind interpretations were truer than our harsh ones? What mistakes have we not made in judging others! But have they not almost always been on the side of harshness? Every day some phenomenon of this kind occurs. We have seen a thing as clear as day. It could have but one meaning. We have already taken measures. We have roused our righteous indignation. All at once the whole matter is differently explained, and that in some most simple way, so simple that we are lost in astonishment that we should never have thought of it ourselves. Always distrust very plain cases, says a legal writer. Things that were dark begin to give light. What seemed opaque is perceived to be transparent. Things that everybody differed about, as people in planting a tree can never agree what it wants to make it straight, now everyone sees in the same light, so natural and obvious has the explanation been. Nay, things that it appeared impossible to explain are just those the explanation of which are the most simple.

How many times in life have we been wrong when we put a kind construction on the conduct of others? We shall not need our fingers to count those mistakes upon. Moreover, grace is really much more common than our querulousness is generally willing to allow. We may suspect its operations in the worst men we meet with. Thus, without any forced impossibility, we may call in supernatural considerations to make our criticisms more ingenious in their charity. When we grow a little holier, we shall summon also to our aid those supernatural motives in ourselves which, by depressing our own ideas of ourselves, elevate our generous belief in others.

But while common sense convinces us of the truth of kind interpretations, common selfishness ought to open our eyes to their wisdom and their policy. We must have passed through life unobservantly if we have never perceived that a man is very much himself what he thinks of others. Of course, his own faults may be the cause of his unfavorable judgments of others; but they are also, and in a very marked way, effects of those same judgments. A man who was on a higher eminence before will soon by harsh judgments of others sink to the level of his own judgments. When you hear a man attribute meanness to another, you may be sure, not only that the critic is an ill-natured man, but that he has got a similar element of meanness in himself or is fast sinking to it. A man is always capable himself of a sin which he thinks another is capable of, or which he himself is capable of imputing to another. Even a well-founded suspicion more or less degrades a man. His suspicion may be verified, and he may escape some material harm by having cherished the suspicion. But he is unavoidably the worse man in consequence of having entertained it. ₰This is a very serious consideration, and rather a frightening argument in favor of charitable interpretations. Furthermore, our hidden judgments of others are, almost with a show of special and miraculous interference, visited upon ourselves. Virtue grows in us under the influence of kindly judgments, as if they were its nutriment. But in the case of harsh judgments, we find we often fall into the sin of which we have judged another guilty, although it is not perhaps a sin at all common to ourselves. Or, if matters do not go so far as this, we find ourselves suddenly overwhelmed with a tempest of unusual temptations, and on reflection conscience is ready to remind us that the sin to which we are thus violently and unexpectedly tempted is one which we have of late been uncharitably attributing to others. Sometimes also we are ourselves falsely accused and widely believed to be guilty of some fault of which we are quite innocent; but it is a fault of which we have recently, in our mind at least, accused another. Moreover, the truth or falsehood of our judgments seem to have very little to do with the matter. The truth of them does not protect us from their unpleasant consequences; just as the truth of a libel is no sufficient defense of it. It is the uncharitableness of the judgment, or the judging at all, to which this self avenging power is fastened. It works itself out like a law, quietly but infallibly. Is not this matter for very serious reflection?

But, in conclusion, what does all this doctrine of kind interpretations amount to? To nothing less, in the case of most of us, than living a new life in a new world. We may imagine life in another planet, with whose physical laws we may happen to have a sufficient acquaintance. But it would hardly differ more in a physical way from our earthly life, than our moral life would differ from what it is at present, if we were habitually to put a kind interpretation on all we saw and heard, and habitually had kind thoughts of every one of whom we thought at all. It would not merely put a new face on life: it would put a new depth to it. We should come as near as possible to becoming another kind of creatures. Look what an

amount of bitterness we have about us! What is to become of it? It
plainly cannot be taken into heaven. Where must it be left behind?
We clearly cannot put it off by the mere fact of dying, as we can put
off thereby a rheumatic limb, or wasted lungs, or diseased blood. It
will surely be a long and painful process in the heats of purgatory;
but we may be happy if mercy so abound upon us that the weight of
our bitterness shall not sink us deeper into the fire, into that depth
from which no one ever rises to the surface more. But when we
reach heaven, in what state shall we be? Certainly, one very important
feature of it will be the absence of all bitterness and criticism, and the
way in which our expanded minds will be possessed with thoughts
of the most tender and overflowing kindness. Thus, by cultivating
kind thoughts we are in a very special way rehearsing for heaven.
But more than this: we are effectually earning heaven. For by God's
grace we are imitating in our own minds that which in the Divine
Mind we rest all our hopes on —merciful allowances, ingeniously
favorable interpretations, thoughts of unmingled kindness, and all the
inventions and tolerations of a supreme compassion.

The practice of kind thoughts also tells most decisively on our
spiritual life. It leads to great self-denial about our talents and
influence. Criticism is an element in our reputation, and an item in
our influence. We partly attract people to us by it. We partly push
principles by means of it. The practice of kind thoughts commits
us to the surrendering of all this. It makes us, again and again in
life, sacrifice successes at the moment they are within our reach. Our
conduct becomes a perpetual voluntary forfeiture of little triumphs,
the necessary result of which is a hidden life. He who has ever struggled
with a proud heart and a bitter temper will perceive at once what
innumerable and vast processes of spiritual combat all this implies.
But it brings its reward also. It endows us with a marvelous facility in

spiritual things. It opens and smooths the paths of prayer. It sheds a clear, still light over our self-knowledge. It adds a peculiar delight to the exercise of faith. It enables us to find God easily. It is a fountain of joy in our souls which rarely intermits its flowing, and then only for a little while and for a greater good. Above all things, the practice of kind thoughts is our main help to that complete government of the tongue which we all so much covet, and without which the Apostle says that our religion is vain. The interior beauty of a soul through habitual kindliness of thought is greater than our words can tell. To such a man life is a perpetual bright evening, with all things calm and fragrant and restful. The dust of life is laid, and its fever cool. All sounds are softer, as in the way of evening, and all sights are fairer, and the golden light makes our enjoyment of earth a happily pensive preparation for heaven.

KIND WORDS

From thoughts we naturally pass to words. Kind words are the music of the world. They have a power which seems to be beyond natural causes, as if they were some Angel's song which had lost its way and come on earth and sang on undyingly, smiting the hearts of men with sweetest wounds, and putting for the while an Angel's nature into us.

Let us then think, first of all, of the power of kind words. In truth, there is hardly a power on earth equal to them. It seems as if they could almost do what God alone can do—namely, soften the hard and angry hearts of men. Many a friendship, long, loyal and self-sacrificing, rested at first on no thicker foundation than a kind word. The two men were not likely to be friends. Perhaps each of them regarded the other's antecedents with somewhat of distrust. They had possibly been set against each other by the circulation of gossip. Or they had been looked upon as rivals, and the success of one was regarded as incompatible with the success of the other. But a kind word, perhaps a mere report of a kind word, has been enough to set all things straight, and to be the commencement of an enduring friendship. The power of kind words is shown also in the destruction of prejudices, however inveterate they may have been. Surely, we must all of us have experienced this ourselves. For a long time, we have had prejudices against a person. They seem to be extremely well

founded. We have a complete view of the whole case in our own
mind. Some particular circumstances bring us into connection with
this man. We see nothing to disabuse us of our prejudices. There
is not an approach to any kind of proof, however indirect, that we
were either mistaken in forming such a judgment, or that we have
exaggerated the matter. But kind words pass, and the prejudices thaw
away. Right or wrong, there was some reason or show of reason for
forming them, while there is neither reason nor show of reason for
their departure. There is no logic in the matter, but a power which is
above logic, the simple, unassisted power of a few kind words. What
has been said of prejudices applies equally to quarrels. Kind words will
set right things which have got most intricately wrong. In reality an
unforgiving heart is a rare monster. Most men get tired of the justest
quarrels. Even those quarrels where the quarrel has all been on one
side, and which are always the hardest to set right, give way in time
to kind words. At first they will be unfairly taken as admissions that
we have been in the wrong; then they will be put down to deceit
and flattery; then they will irritate by the discomfort of conscience
which they will produce in the other; but finally they will (Succeed
in healing the wound that has been Iso often and so obstinately torn
open. All quarrels probably rest on misunderstanding, and only live
by silence, which, as it were, stereotypes the misunderstanding. A
misunderstanding which is more than a month old may generally be
regarded as incapable of explanation. Renewed explanations become
renewed misunderstandings. Kind words patiently uttered for long
together, and without visible fruit, are our only hope. They will
succeed; they will not explain what has been misunderstood, but they
will do what is much better—make explanation unnecessary, and so
avoid the risk which always accompanies explanations of reopening
old sores.

In all the foregoing instances the power of kind words is remedial.
But it can be productive also; kind words produce happiness. How
often have we ourselves been made happy by kind words, in a manner
and to an extent which we are quite unable to explain? No analysis
enables us to detect the secret of the power of kind words; even
self-love is found inadequate as a cause. Now, as I have said before,
happiness is a great power of holiness. Thus, kind words, by their
power of producing happiness, have also a power of producing
holiness, and so winning men to God. I have already touched on
this when I spoke of kindness in general, but it must now be added
that words have a power of their own, both for good and evil, which
I believe to be more influential and energetic over our fellow men
than even actions. If I may use such a word when I am speaking of
religious subjects, it is by voice and words that men mesmerize each
other. Hence it is that the world is converted by the foolishness of
preaching. Hence it is that an angry word rankles longer in the heart
than an angry gesture—nay, very often even longer than a blow. Thus,
all that has been said of the power of kindness in general applies
with an additional and peculiar force to kind words. They prepare
men for conversion, they convert them, they sanctify them, they
procure entrance for wholesome counsels into their souls; they blunt
temptations, they dissolve the dangerous clouds of gloom and sadness,
they are beforehand with evil, they exorcise the devil. Sometimes the
conversions they work are gradual and take time; but more often
they are sudden, more often they are like instantaneous revelations
from heaven, not only unravelling complicated misunderstandings,
and softening the hardened conviction of years, but giving a divine
vocation to the soul. Truly it would be worth going through fire and
water to acquire the right and to find the opportunity of saying kind
words! Surely, then, it gives life a peculiar character that it should be

gifted with a power so great, even if the exercise of it were difficult
and rare. But the facility of this power is a fresh wonder about it in
addition to its greatness. It involves very little self-sacrifice, and for
the most part none at all. It can be exercised generally without much
effort, with no more effort than the water makes in flowing from the
spring. Moreover, the occasions for it do not lie scattered over life at
great distances from each other. They occur continually; they come
daily; they are frequent in the day. All these are commonplaces: but
really it would seem as if very few of us give this power of kind words
the consideration which is due to it. So great a power, such a facility in
the exercise of it, such a frequency of opportunities for the application
of it, and yet the world still what it is, and we still what we are! It
seems incredible. I can only compare it to the innumerable sacraments
which inundate our souls with grace, and the inexplicable modicum of
holiness, which is the total result of them all, or, again, to the immense
amount of knowledge of God which there is in the world, and yet the
little worship He receives. Kind words cost us nothing, yet how often
do we grudge them? On the few occasions when they do imply some
degree of self-sacrifice, they almost instantly repay us a hundred-fold.
The opportunities are frequent, but we show no eagerness either
in looking out for them, or in embracing them. What inference are
we to draw from all this? Surely this: That it is next to impossible
to be habitually kind, except by the help of Divine grace and upon
supernatural motives. Take life all through, its adversity as well as its
prosperity, its sickness as well as its health, its loss of its rights as well
as its enjoyment of them, and we shall find that no natural sweetness
of temper, much less any acquired philosophical equanimity, is equal
to the support of a uniform habit of kindness. Nevertheless, with the
help of grace, the habit of saying kind words is very quickly formed,
and when once formed, it is not speedily lost.

I have often thought that unkindness is very much a mental habit, almost as much mental as moral; observation has confirmed me in this idea, because I have met so many men with unkind heads and have been fortunate enough never to my knowledge to have come across an unkind heart. I believe cruelty to be less uncommon than real inward unkindness.

Self-interest makes it comparatively easy for us to do that which we are well paid for doing. The great price which everyone puts on a little kind word makes the practice of saying them still easier. They become easier, the more on the one hand that we know ourselves, and on the other that we are united to God. Yet what are these but the two contemporaneous operations of grace, in which the life of holiness consists? Kindness to be perfect, to be lasting, must be a conscious imitation of God: sharpness, bitterness, sarcasm, acute observation, divination of motives—all these things disappear when a man is earnestly conforming himself to the image of Christ Jesus. The very attempt to be like our dearest Lord is already a well-spring of sweetness within us, flowing with an easy grace over all who come within our reach. It is true that a special sort of unkindness is one of the uglinesses of pious beginnings. But this arises from our inability to manage our fresh grace properly. Our old bitterness gets the impulse meant for our sweetness, and the machine cannot be got right in a moment. He who is not patient with converts to God will forfeit many of his own graces before he is aware. Not only is kindness due to everyone, but a special kindness is due to everyone. Kindness is not kindness unless it be special; it is in its fitness, seasonableness, and individual application, that its charm consists.

It is natural to pass from the facility of kind words to its reward. I find myself always talking about happiness when I am treating of kindness. The fact is the two things go together; the double reward

of kind words is in the happiness they cause in others and the
happiness they cause in ourselves. The very process of uttering them
is a happiness in itself. Even the imagining of them fills our minds
with sweetness, and makes our hearts glow pleasurably. Is there any
happiness in the world like the happiness of a disposition made happy
by the happiness of others? There is no joy to be compared with it.
The luxuries which wealth can buy, the rewards which ambition can
attain, the pleasures of art and scenery, the abounding sense of health,
and the exquisite enjoyment of mental creations, are nothing to this
pure and heavenly happiness, where self is drowned in the blessedness
of others. Yet this happiness follows close upon kind words and is
their legitimate result. But, independently of this, kind words make
us happy in ourselves. They soothe our own irritation, they charm our
cares away, they draw us nearer to God, they raise the temperature of
our love. They produce in us a sense of quiet restfulness like that which
accompanies the consciousness of forgiven sin. They shed abroad the
peace of God within our hearts. Then, moreover, we become kinder by
saying kind words, and this is in itself a third reward. They help us also
to attain the grace of purity, which is another excellent reward. They
win us many other graces from God; but one especially: they appear
to have a peculiar congeniality with the grace of contrition, which is
softheartedness towards God. Everything which makes us gentle has
at the same time a tendency to make us contrite. A natural melting of
the heart has often been the beginning of an acceptable repentance.
Hence it is that seasons of sorrow are apt to be seasons of grace. This,
too, is a huge reward. Then, last of all, kind words make us truthful.
Oh, this is what we want to be true! It is our insincerity, our manifold
inseparable falseness, which is the load under which we groan. There
is no slavery but untruthfulness. How have years passed in fighting,
and still, we are so untrue! It clings to us; for it is the proper stain of

creatures. We fight on wearily; kind words come and ally themselves to us, and we make way. They make us true, because kindness is, so far as we know, the most probable truth in the world. They make us true because what is untruthful is not kind. They make us true, because kindness is God's view, and His view is already the true view.

Why, then, are we ever anything else but kind in our words? There are some difficulties. This must be honestly admitted. In some respects, a clever man is more likely to be kind than a man who is not clever, because his mind is wider, and takes in a broader range, and is more capable of looking at things from different points of view. But there are other respects in which it is harder for a clever man to be kind, especially in his words. He has a temptation, and it is one of those temptations which appear sometimes to border on the irresistible, to say clever things; and, somehow, clever things are hardly ever kind things. There is a drop either of acid or of bitter in them, and it seems as if that drop was exactly what genius had insinuated. I believe, if we were to make an honest resolution never to say a clever thing, we should advance much more rapidly on the road to heaven. Our Lord's words in the Gospels should be our models.

If we may reverently say it, when we consider of what a sententious and proverbial character His words were, it is remarkable how little of epigram or sharpness there is in them. Of course, the words of the Eternal Word are all of them heavenly mysteries, each one with the light and seal of His Divinity upon it. At the same time, they are also examples to us. Overall, to say clever things of others is hardly ever without sin. There is something in genius which is analogous to a sting. Its sharpness, its speed, its delicacy, its wantonness, its pain and its poison, genius has all these things as well as the sting. There are some men who make it a kind of social profession to be amusing talkers. One is sometimes overwhelmed with melancholy by their professional efforts to be entertaining. They are the bugbears of real conversation. But the thing to notice about them here is, that they can hardly ever be religious men. A man who lays himself out to amuse is never a safe man to have for a friend, or even for an acquaintance. He is not a man whom anyone really loves or respects. He is never innocent. He is forever jostling charity by the pungency of his criticisms, and wounding justice by the revelation of secrets. 'Il n'est pas ordinaire,' says La Bruyere, 'qui celui qui fait rire, se fasse estimer.'

There is also a grace of kind listening, as well as a grace of kind speaking. Some men listen with an abstracted air, which shows that their thoughts are elsewhere. Or they seem to listen, but by wide answers and irrelevant questions show that they have been occupied with their own thoughts, as being more interesting, at least in their own estimation, than what you were saying. Some listen with a kind of importunate ferocity, which makes you feel that you have been put on your trial, and that your auditor expects beforehand that you are going to tell him a lie, or to be inaccurate, or to say something which he will disapprove, and that you must mind your expressions. Some interrupt and will not hear you to the end. Some hear you to the end, and then forthwith begin to speak to you of a similar experience which has befallen themselves, making your case only an illustration of their own. Some, meaning to be kind, listen with such a determined, lively, violent attention that you are at once made uncomfortable, and the charm of conversation is at an end. Many persons whose manners will stand the test of speaking, break down under the trial of listening. But all these things ought to be brought under the sweet influences of religion. Kind listening is often an act of the most delicate interior mortification and is a great assistance towards kind speaking. Those who govern others must take care to be kind listeners, or else they will soon offend God and fall into secret sins.

We may, then, put down clever speeches as the first and greatest difficulty in the way of kind words. A second difficulty is that of repressing vexation at certain times and in certain places. Each man meets with peculiar characters who have a specialty, often quite inexplicable, of irritating him. They always come at the wrong time, say the most inopportune things, and make the most unfortunate choice of topics of conversation. Their presence always has something intrusive about it. You may admire, respect, even like, the persons, yet you give out sparks when they touch you, and explode if they rub against you. This is only one example of many species of vexation, which it is difficult to repress in our social intercourse, and which it is the office of the spirit of kindness to allay.

The unselfishness of speedily and gracefully distracting ourselves from self is also singularly difficult to practice. A man comes to us with an imaginary sorrow when we are bowed to the earth with a real one. Or he speaks to us with the loud voice and metallic laugh of robust health, when our nerves are all shrinking up with pain, and our whole being quivering, like a mimosa, with excruciating sensitiveness. Or he comes to pour out the exuberance of his happiness into our hearts which are full of gloom, and his brightness is a reproach, sometimes almost a menace, to our happiness. Or we are completely possessed with some responsibility, harassed by some pecuniary difficulty, or haunted by some tyrannical presentiment of evil, and yet we are called upon to throw ourselves into some ridiculous little embarrassment, some almost fictitious wrong, or some shadow of a suffering, for which another claims our sympathy. Here is a grand material for sanctification. Nevertheless, such materials are hard to work up in practice. It is weary work cleaning old bricks to build a new house with.

These are difficulties, but we have got to reach heaven and must push on. The more humble we are, the more kindly we shall talk; the more kindly we talk, the more humble we shall grow. An air of superiority is foreign to the genius of kindness. The look of kindness is that of one receiving a favor rather than conferring it. Indeed, it is the case with all the virtues, that kindness is a road to them. Kind words will help us to them. Thus, out of the difficulties of kind speaking will come the grand and more than sufficient reward of kind speaking, a sanctification higher, completer, swifter, easier, than any other sanctification.

Weak and full of wants as we are ourselves, we must make up our minds, or rather take heart, to do some little good to this poor world while we are in it. Kind words are our chief implements for this work. A kind-worded man is a genial man; and geniality is power. Nothing sets wrong right so soon as geniality. There are a thousand things to be reformed, and no reform succeeds unless it be genial. No one was ever corrected by a sarcasm, crushed, perhaps, if the sarcasm was clever enough, but drawn nearer to God, never. Men want to advocate changes, it may be in politics, or in science, or in philosophy, or in literature, or perhaps in the working of the Church. They give lectures, they write books, they start reviews, they found schools to propagate their views, they coalesce in associations, they collect money, they move reforms in public meetings, and all to further their peculiar ideas. They are unsuccessful. From being unsuccessful themselves, they become unsympathetic with others. From this comes narrowness of mind; their very talents are deteriorated. The next step is to be snappish, then bitter, then eccentric, then rude. After that they abuse people for not taking their advice; and, last of all, their impotence, like that of all angry prophets, ends in the shrillness of a scream. Why they scream is not so obvious. Perhaps for their own relief. It is the frenzy of the disregarded Sibyl. All this comes of their not being genial. Without geniality no solid reform was ever made yet. But if there are a thousand things to reform in the world, there are tens of thousands of people to convert. Satire will not convert men. Hell threatened very kindly is more persuasive than a biting truth about a man's false position. The fact is geniality is the best controversy. The genial man is the only successful man. Nothing can be done for God without geniality. More plans fail for want of that than for the want of anything else. A genial man is both an apostle and an evangelist—an apostle because he brings men to Christ; an evangelist because he portrays Christ to men.

KIND ACTIONS

There is always one bright thought in our minds when all the rest is dark. There is one thought out of which a moderately cheerful man can always make some satisfactory sunshine, if not a sufficiency of it. It is the thought of the bright populous heaven. There is a joy there at least, if there is a joy nowhere else. There is true service of God there, however poor and interested the love of Him may be on earth. Multitudes are abounding in the golden light there, even if they that rejoice on earth be few. At this hour it is all going on so near us that we cannot be hopelessly unhappy with so much happiness so near. Yet its nearness makes us wistful. Then let us think that there are multitudes in heaven today who are there because of kind actions; many are there for doing them, many for having had them done to them.

We cannot do justice to the subject of kindness if we conclude without saying something about kind actions and kind suffering. So let us think, first of all, how much we ourselves owe in past life to kind actions. If we look back through the last twenty or thirty years, it is amazing to consider the number of kind actions that have been done to us; they are almost beyond our counting. Indeed, we feel that those we remember are hardly so numerous as those we have forgotten—forgotten not through ingratitude, but because of the distractions of life and the shortness of our memory, lender what

various circumstances too, they have been done to us! They have come
to us together with blame, as well as been the accompaniments of
praise. They have made our darkness light, and our light brighter.
They have made us smile in the midst of our tears and have made us
shed tears of joy when we were laughing carelessly. They have come to
us also from all quarters. They have reached us through people whom
we might have expected to meet them. They have reached us from
unexpected people who would naturally have been indifferent to us.
They have reached us from those from whom we had every reason to
expect the opposite. They have come to us from such unhoped - for
quarters, and under such an affecting variety of circumstances, that
each one of us must have seemed to himself to have exhausted the
possibilities of kindness. The thought of them all melts our hearts.

Now, every one of those acts of kindness has doubtless done us
a certain amount of spiritual good. If they did not make us better
at the time, they prepared the way for our becoming better, or they
sowed a seed of future goodness, and made an impression which we
never suspected, and yet which was ineffaceable. Graces from God,
kindnesses from men; we seem to have stood all our lives under the
beneficent drippings of these beneficent showers. But who can say if
there were two showers, and if it was not all the while but one, kindness
being nothing more than a peculiar form of grace? There is no great
harm in confounding the two; but to be strict, grace is one thing, and
kindness is another.

Let us content ourselves, then, with saying that kindness has again
and again done the preliminary work for grace in our souls. Let us
think also how little we have deserved all these kind actions, not only so
far as God is concerned, but so far as our fellow creatures are concerned
also. There is no one who has not received tenfold more kindness
himself than he has shown to others. The thought of all the kindness

of so many persons to us sometimes grows to be almost intolerable because of the sense of our own unkindness. These kind actions have been to us like importunate Angels. They have surrounded us almost against our own will, and done us all manner of unasked good, of extra good, of good apparently unconnected with themselves. From how many evils have they not also rescued us? We know of many, but there are many more of which we do not know. But in this respect, as well as in others, they have done Angels' work in our behalf. To how much good have they encouraged us? We know much, but there is much more of which we do not know. We can hardly tell what we should have been had we been treated one whit less kindly than we have been. Have we not sometimes been on the verge of doing something which a life would have been short to repent of? Have not words been on our tongues which, had we said them, we would willingly have lost a limb afterwards to have unsaid? Have we not vacillated in the face of decisions which we now perceive to concern eternity as well as time? Can we not now see in retrospect steep places down which we were beginning to fall, and a kind act saved us, and at the time we thought we had stumbled over a stone by the way? We are indeed very far from what we ought to be now. But it is frightening to think what we might have been had parents, friends, nurses, masters, servants, schoolfellows, enemies, been less kind than they have been. All through life kindness has been bridling the devil that was in us. The surprised and affectionate recollection of it now is one of our greatest powers for virtue and may easily be made a fountain of interior sweetness within ourselves. Feeling that we ourselves owe all this to the kindness of others, are we not bound, as far as lies in our power, to be putting everyone else on all sides of us under similarly blessed obligations?

It is not hard to do this. The occasions for kind actions are
manifold. No one passes a day without meeting these fortunate
opportunities. They grow round us even when we lie on a bed of
sickness, and the helpless are rich in a power of kindness towards the
helpful. Yet, as is always the rule with kindness, the frequency of its
opportunities is rivalled by the facility of its execution. Hardly out of
twenty kind actions does one call for an effort of self-denial on our
part. Easiness is the rule, and difficulty the exception. When kindness
does call for an effort, how noble and self-rewarding is the sacrifice!
We always gain more than we lose; we gain outwardly, and often
even in kind. But the inward gain is invariable; nothing forfeits that.
Moreover, there is something very economical about the generosity of
kindness. A little goes a long way; it seems to be an almost universal
fallacy among mankind, which leads them to put a higher price on
kindness than it deserves. Neither do men look generally at what we
have had to give up in order to do for them what we have done. They
only look to the kindness; the manner is more to them than the matter;
the sacrifice adds something, but only a small proportion of the whole.
The very world, unkindly as it is, looks at kindness through a glass
which multiplies as well as magnifies. I called this a fallacy; it is a sweet
fallacy, and reminds us of that apparent fallacy which leads God to
put such a price upon the pusillanimities of our love. This fallacy,
however, confers upon kind actions a real power. The amount of
kindness bears no proportion to the effect of kindness. The least kind
action is taller than the hugest wrong. The weakest kindness can lift
a heavy weight; it reaches far, and it travels swiftly. Every kind action
belongs to many persons and lays many persons under obligations.
We appropriate to ourselves kind actions done to those we love, and
we forthwith proceed to love the doers of them. Nobody is kind only
to one person at once, but to many people in one. What a beautiful

entanglement of charity we get ourselves into by doing kind things! What possesses us that we do not do them oftener?

Neither is a kind action short-lived. The doing of it is only the beginning of it; it is hardly the thing itself. Years of estrangement can hardly take the odor out of a good action. Hatred, truly, has a chemistry of its own, by which it can turn kind actions into its choicest food. But, after all, hatred is an uncommon thing as well as a brutal one—that is to say, comparatively uncommon; whereas, it is not an uncommon thing for a man at the end of half a century to do a kind action because one was done to him fifty years ago. There is also this peculiarity about kind actions, that the more we try to repay them, the further off we seem to have repaid them. The obligation lengthens, and widens, and deepens. We hasten to fill up the chasm by our gratitude; but we only deepen it, as if we were digging a well or sinking a pit. We go faster still; the abyss grows more hungry; at last our lives become delightfully committed to be nothing but a profusion of kind actions, and we fly heavenwards on the wings of the wind. There is a pathetic sweetness about gratitude which I suppose arises from this. It is a pathos which is very humbling, but very invigorating also. What was the father in the poet's mind to these exquisite verses?

> 'I've heard of hearts unkind, kind deeds
>
> With coldness still returning;
>
> Alas! the gratitude of men
>
> Hath oftener left me mourning!'

But by this time an objection to the whole matter will have come plainly into view. Indeed, to some it has already presented itself before now. I have been aware of it throughout but have chosen to defer noticing it till now. It may be said that all this implies a very unsupernatural view of the spiritual life, and lays undue stress on what are almost natural virtues, that it refers more to outward conduct than to inward experiences, that there is too much of common-sense in it, and too little of mystical theology. I might content myself with replying that a man cannot write on more than one subject at once, neither can he bring in the whole of ascetical doctrine when he is illustrating but one portion of it. But there is something more in the objection; which I can only answer by pleading guilty to the charge, and refusing to be ashamed of my guilt. When we read the lives of the saints, or ponder on the teaching of mystical books, we shall surely have no difficulty in admitting that we ourselves are but beginners, or at least men of very low attainments in the matter of perfection. As such, we are liable to two mistakes; I hardly know whether to call them temptations or delusions. The first is to think too little of external things. Do not misunderstand me. I am not accusing you of paying too much attention to the cultivation of an interior spirit. It is not easy to do this. In our state perhaps it is impossible. But what I mean is, that beginners like to turn their eye away from outward conduct to the more hidden processes of their own spiritual experiences. If we allow a beginner to choose his own subject for particular examen of conscience, he will generally choose some very delicate and imperceptible fault, the theatre of which is almost wholly within, or some refined form of self-love whose metamorphoses are exceedingly difficult either to detect or to control. He will not choose his temper, or his tongue, or his love of nice dishes, or some unworthy habit which is disagreeable to those around him; yet this is the rule of St. Ignatius, and surely no one will accuse him of not cultivating an interior spirit. This, then, is the first of the two mistakes which I attributed to men of low attainments. They affect those parts of the spiritual life which lie on the borders of mystical theology and do justice neither to the common things of the faith nor to the regulation of outward conduct. This leads to hardness of heart, to spiritual pride, and to self-righteousness. It has a peculiar power to neutralize the operations of grace, and to reduce our spirituality to a matter of words and feelings. A man will remain unimproved for years who travels upon this path.

The second mistake is genuinely like the first, though there is a difference in it. It consists in giving way to an attraction which is too high for us. It is not that we divide things into outward and inward and exaggerate the latter. But we divide them into high and commonplace and are inclined almost to despise the latter. We fasten with a sort of diseased eagerness upon the exceptional practices of the saints. Peculiarities have a kind of charm for us. We try to force ourselves to thirst for suffering when we have hardly grace enough for the quiet endurance of a headache. We ask leave to pray for calumny when a jocose retort puts us in a passion. We turn from the Four Last Things as subjects of prayer hardly suited to our state of disinterested love. We skip like antelopes over the purgative way, as if none but the herbage of the illuminative, or the desert flowers of the unitive way, were food delicate enough for us. We enjoy Father Baker very much while we think Rodriguez dry. In a word, we traffic with exceptions rather than with rules. Hence the common moral virtues, the ordinary motives of religion, the duties of our state of life, our responsibilities toward others, the usual teaching of sermons and spiritual books, are kept in the background. We are too well instructed to speak evil of them, or to show them contempt, but we treat them with a respectful neglect. Thus, our spiritual life becomes a sort of elegant selfish solitude, a temple reared to dainty delusions, a mete fastidious and exclusive worship of self whose refinement is only an aggravation of its dishonesty. No saint ever went along this road. We can only reach the delicate truths of mysticism through the commonplace sincerities of asceticism. We are never so likely to be high in the spiritual life as when we are just like everybody else.

The grace to be indistinguishable from the good people round us is a greater grace than that which visibly marks us off from their practices or their attainments.

Now, I believe that both these mistakes find an utterance in the objection which I have noticed, and therefore, as being peculiarly out of sympathy with both these errors, I willingly plead guilty to the objection. I do think we are all in danger of making away with the supernatural by having first used it to destroy the natural. I could go on for hours illustrating this mischievous tendency; but I must keep to my subject, and endeavor to show those who feel they cannot throw off the objection so lightly as I do, what a very real connection there is between this practice of kindness on supernatural motives, and the highest department of the spiritual life. Indeed, it would be difficult to exaggerate the importance of kindness as an ally in our invisible warfare. Naturalists say of the ant that the most surprising part of its instinct is its genius for extemporaneousness. In other words, it almost puts reason to shame, by the promptitude with which it acts under totally new circumstances, its inventiveness in meeting with difficulties of which it can have had no previous experience, its ingenuity in changing the use of its tools, its power of instantaneous divination as to how it shall act in unexpected conjunctures, and its far-seeing judgment in hardly ever having to make an experiment, or to try two ways of doing a thing. Now, there is something very like this in kindness. Spiritual persons who specially cultivate kindness are singularly exempt from delusions. Yet delusions form the most intricate and baffling part of our spiritual warfare. But the instinct of kindness is never baffled. No position ever seems new to it, no difficulty unforeseen. It appears to be dispensed from the necessity of deliberating. It follows the lightninglike changes of self-love or of the temper with a speed as lightning-like as their own. It sees through all stratagems. It is forever extemporizing new methods of defense and new varieties of attack. It always has light enough to work by because it is luminous itself.

Besides this, kindness has an intrinsic congeniality with all the characteristics of the higher spiritual states. Kind actions go upon unselfish motives, and therefore tend to form a habit of disinterestedness in us, which prepares us for the highest motives of Divine love. They also catch us up, like strong Angels, into the regions of sacrifice. Like God's goodness, they are constantly occupied where there is no hope of payment and return. Like the shedding of the Precious Blood, they have an actual preference for multiplying themselves upon their enemies. In like manner as God acts evermore for His own glory, so kind actions, when they are habitual, must very frequently be done for Him alone. It is their instinct to be hidden, like the instinct of His providence. Nay, God often rewards them by arranging that they shall be unrequited, and so look only to Him as Himself their recompense; and He shows frequently a most tender wisdom in arranging that all this shall be without the sin or ingratitude of others. He even shrouds our kind actions for us by letting us look stern or speak sharply or be quick-tempered in the doing of them. I need not stop to develop all this. Who does not see that we are here right in the midst of the motive-machinery of the very highest spiritual condition of the soul?

It may not be out of place, however, to lay down a few plain rules for the doing of kind actions. I have said that the majority of them require no effort; but when they have to be done with effort, it is unkind not to keep the effort out of view. At the same time, so that our humility may not be disquieted, we must bear in mind that the being done with effort is no just cause of disheartenment. We should never repeat to others our good actions. If we do, their heavenly influence over ourselves goes at once. Neither does it simply evaporate; it remains as a dead weight. The soul has many heaps of rubbish in it, but none more deleterious than this. When men begin to thank us, we should playfully stop their thanks, but not stiffly or unreally. There are some men who would feel awkward and uncomfortable if they were not allowed to pour out their feelings. Such men we must not check. It is part of the discernment of good manners to find out who they are, and the perfection of good manners to be natural and simple under the operation of being praised. Being praised puts us for the most part in a ludicrous position. Either it mortifies us by a sense of inferiority, or it makes us suspicious by a feeling of disproportion, or it unseasonably awakes our sense of humor, which is always in proportion to the honest seriousness of those who are praising us. The fact is, very few people know how to praise, and fewer still know how to take it. We should never dwell upon our kind actions in our own minds. God is in them. They have been operations of grace. God is shy of being looked at and withdraws. When we are tempted to be complacent about them, let us think of the sanctity of God and be ashamed. Let us dwell on His attribute of magnificence and be especially devout to it. We shall thus keep ourselves within the limits of our own littleness, and even feel comfortable in them.

Before we conclude our task, we must say something about kind suffering. Kind suffering is, in fact, a form of kind action, with peculiar rubrics of its own. But if all kindness needs grace, kind suffering needs it a hundredfold. Of a truth those are rare natures which know how to suffer gracefully, and in whose endurance there is a natural beauty which simulates, and sometimes even seems to surpass, what is supernatural. To the Christian, no sight is melancholier than this simulating of grace by nature. It is a problem which makes him thoughtful, but to which no thinking brings a satisfactory solution. With the Christian kind suffering must be almost wholly supernatural. It is a region in which grace must be despotic, so despotic as hardly to allow nature to dwell in the land. There is a harmonious fusion of suffering and gentleness effected by grace, which is one of the most attractive features of holiness. With quiet and unobtrusive sweetness, the sufferer makes us feel as if he were ministering to us rather than we to him. It is we who are under the obligation. To wait on him is a privilege rather than a task. Even the softening, sanctifying influences of suffering seem to be exercising themselves on us rather than on him. His gentleness makes us gentle. He casts a spell over us. We have all the advantages of being his inferiors without being vexed with a sense of our inferiority. What is more beautiful than considerateness for others when we ourselves are unhappy? It is a grace made out of a variety of graces, and yet while it makes a deep impression on all who come within the sphere of its influence, it is a very hidden grace. It is part of those deep treasures of the heart which the world can seldom rifle.

To be subject to low spirits is a sad liability. Yet, to a vigorous, manly heart, it may be a very complete sanctification. What can be more unkind than to communicate our low spirits to others, to go about the world like demons, poisoning the fountains of joy? Have I more light because I have managed to involve those I love in the same gloom as myself? Is it not pleasant to see the sun shining on the mountains, even though we have none of it down in our valley? Oh, the littleness and the meanness of that sickly appetite for sympathy which will not let us keep our tiny Lilliputian sorrows to ourselves! Why must we go sneaking about, like some dishonorable insect, and feed our darkness on other people's light? We hardly know in all this whether to be more disgusted with the meanness, or more indignant at the selfishness, or more sorrowful at the sin. The thoughts of the dying mother are all concentrated on her newborn child. It is a beautiful emblem of unselfish holiness. So also let us hide our pains and sorrows. But while we hide them, let them also be spurs within us to urge us on to all manner of overflowing kindness and sunny humor to those around us. When the very darkness within us creates a sunshine around us, then has the Spirit of Jesus taken possession of our souls.

Social contact has something irritating in it, even when it is kindliest. Those who love us are continually aggravating us, not only unintentionally, but even in the display of their love. Unkindness also abounds and is of itself vexatious. Something goes wrong daily. It is difficult even for sympathy not to exasperate. Consolation is almost always chafing. We often seem to have come into the world without our skins, so that all intercourse is agony to our sensitivity. What a field for sanctification all this opens out to us! Then there is another sort of sweetness under God's visitations, and this shows itself especially in taking all the burden we can off others. For the fact is, that everybody's cross is shared by many. No one carries his own cross wholly; at least, such crosses are very rare. I am not quite sure that they exist. Now, kind suffering makes us habitually look rather at what others feel of our crosses than of what we feel of them ourselves. We see our own crosses on other people's shoulders and overwhelm them with kindness accordingly. It is not we who have been tossing wakeful all night that are the sufferers, but the poor nurse who has been fighting all night against the sleep of health by our bedside, and only with partial success. It is not we who cannot bear the least noise in the house that deserve sympathy, but the poor little constrained children who have not been allowed to make the noise. For to children is there any happiness which is not also noise? This is the turn of mind which kind suffering gives us. Who will say it is not a most converting thing? But then, it must develop itself gracefully. We must do all this unobtrusively, so as not to let others see it is done on purpose. Hence it is that the saints keep silence in suffering; for the mere knowledge of what they suffer is itself a suffering to those who love them. But suffering is a world of miracles. It would fill a book to say all that might be said about kindness under suffering.

Let us conclude. We have been speaking of kindness. Perhaps we might better have called it the spirit of Jesus. What an amulet we should find it in our passage through life if we would say to ourselves two or three times a day these soft words of Scripture: 'My spirit is sweet above honey, and my inheritance above honey and the honeycomb.' But you will say perhaps: 'After all, it is a very little virtue, very much a matter of natural temperament, and rather an affair of good manners than of holy living.' Well, I will not argue with you. The grass of the fields is better than the cedars of Lebanon. It feeds more, and it rests the eye better— that thymy, daisy - eyed carpet, making earth sweet, and fair, and homelike. Kindness is the turf of the spiritual world, whereon the sheep of Christ feed quietly beneath the Shepherd's eye.

'It was only a sunny smile, And little it cost in the giving;

But it scattered the night Like morning light,

And made the day worth living,

Through life's dull warp a woof it wove

In shining colors of hope and love;

And the Angels smiled as they watched above,

Yet little it cost in the giving.

'It was but a kindly word,

A word that was lightly spoken;

Yet not in vain,

For it stilled the pain
Of a heart that was nearly broken.
It strengthened a faith beset with fears,
And groping blindly through mists of tears,
For light to brighten the coming years,
Although it was lightly spoken.
'It was only a helping hand,
And it seemed of little availing;
But its clasp was warm,
And it saved from harm
A brother whose strength was failing.
Its touch was tender as angels' wings,
But it rolled the stone from the hidden springs,
And pointed the way to higher things,
Though it seemed of little availing.'

Anon.

THE END